Seafood

Fish is an important source of protein in the diets of people all over the world. This book takes a look at the world's fishing industry – from how fish are found, caught, processed and sold, to the problems of pollution, conservation, and dividing up our oceans into fishing areas. Harry Barrett is a trade journalist who has specialized in writing about the fishing industry. During the past ten years he has travelled extensively around the world, gaining knowledge of the way different nations have developed their fisheries.

Focus on
SEAFOOD

Harry Barrett

Wayland

Focus on Resources series

Alternative Energy
Coal
Coffee
Cotton
Dairy Produce
Fruit
Gas
Gold and Silver
Grain
Iron and Steel
Meat
Nuclear Fuel
Oil
Paper
Plastics
Rice
Rubber
Seafood
Soya
Sugar
Tea
Timber
Water
Wool

Frontispiece *The Argunda fishing festival in Nigeria.*

First published in 1986 by
Wayland (Publishers) Ltd
61 Western Road, Hove
East Sussex BN3 1JD, England

Phototypeset by Kalligraphics Ltd, Redhill, Surrey
Printed and bound in Italy by G. Canale & C.S.p.A., Turin

British Library Cataloguing in Publication Data
Barrett, Harry
Focus on seaford. – (Focus on resources series)
1. Fisheries – Juvenile literature
I. Title II. Series
338.3′727092 SH331.15

ISBN 0–85078–656–8

Contents

1.	A giant 'food bowl'	*6*
2.	How we get food from the sea	*8*
3.	Finding fish	*10*
4.	The main fishing methods	*12*
5.	Fishing boats of the world	*14*
6.	Keeping fish fresh	*16*
7.	Buying and selling seafood	*18*
8.	Dividing up the sea	*20*
9.	Policing the sea	*22*
10.	Sharing out the fish	*24*
11.	Top fishing nations	*26*
12.	Seafood and health	*28*
13.	Farming fish	*30*
14.	Fisheries and research	*32*
15.	Changing one fish into another	*34*
16.	Different tastes	*36*
17.	The wonderful world of shellfish	*38*
18.	Sharing the sea	*40*
19.	Keeping the sea clean	*42*
	Facts and figures	*44*
	Glossary	*46*
	Sources of further information	*46*
	Books to read	*47*
	Index	*48*

1. A giant 'food bowl'

Over 70 million tonnes of fish are now taken out of the sea every year. Fish are hunted in every ocean of the world. By the year 2000, the world catch will have to rise to 100 million tonnes a year, if there is to be enough protein to feed all the extra people there will be on earth.

With two-thirds of the earth covered by water, the sea has played an important part in

The varied catch of a prawn trawler in the Gulf of Carpentaria.

Above *A skilful form of fishing in Sri Lanka.*

the development of civilization. People first used the sea as a means of travel, but it was not long before they discovered that it was also an important source of food.

From finding that fish washed up on the shore were good to eat, early humans first started hunting fish in the way they had learned to hunt animals on the land: using spears. Soon they found an easier way to catch fish was to set traps (small barriers) which left fish stranded on the shore when the tide went out.

Lines and hooks, baited with food that fish like to eat, came next. Then humans discovered that by using nets, they could take enormous quantities of fish out of the sea. Today one single dip of a net can trap 100 tonnes of fish.

Humankind has now become so clever at hunting in the sea that soon there may not be enough fish left to catch.

Every country in the world, which has a coastline, now hunts fish. These fishing nations are working together to make sure there will be enough fish for the future. This is called 'conservation' and later on in this book you will see how this is being carried out.

Below *This mosaic shows the importance of fish in the lives of ancient people.*

2. How we get food from the sea

Fishermen have been very clever at finding ways to get food out of the sea. They have used electric currents to stun fish, giant suction machines to 'hoover' them out of the water and undersea cages to trap them. To catch the largest of all sea creatures – the whale – a harpoon is used. This is a spear fired from a gun.

Getting fish out of the sea is only half the job. Often fish have to be lured into places where fishermen can catch them. Many fishermen in the Mediterranean and Latin American countries use powerful lights hung out from their boats, which the fish follow.

Chemicals, which give off a smell that fish like, are sometimes used. Another method is to put female fish in baskets in the water to attract male fish.

A suction pump can be used to catch fish.

Building an artificial reef from tyres.

Even old cars and rubber tyres have a use in catching fish. Fishermen drop these into the sea to make artificial wrecks and reefs, around which fish like to swim and feed.

If the price of oil continues to go up, ways of herding fish into one place will become more important. Pulling fishing nets long distances through the water, by boat, uses a lot of fuel and often means that a fisherman loses money on his catch. Some fishermen have tried going back to using sails to propel their boats.

Whales have to be killed with harpoon guns.

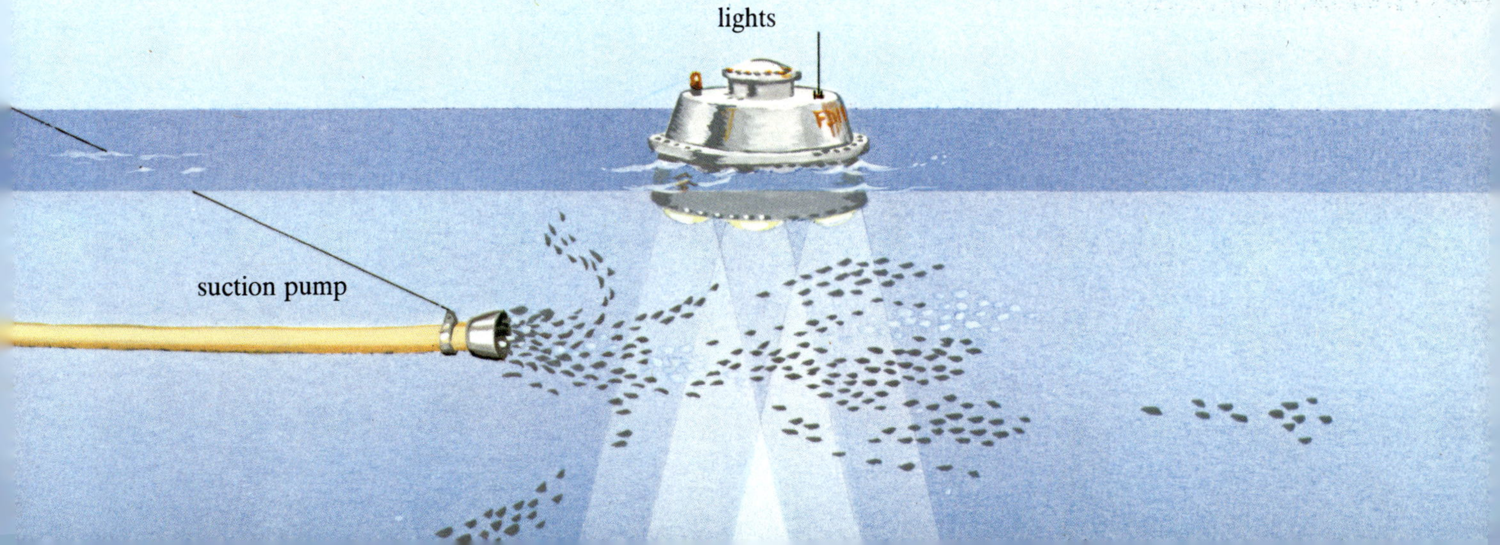

3. Finding fish

The wheelhouse of a modern fishing boat is like the cockpit of an aeroplane: rows and rows of instruments and dials.

A fisherman relies on modern electronic equipment to help him find his way around the ocean and to find fish. This equipment has become so efficient that it can 'see' a single fish 1,600 metres (5,280 feet) down in the ocean.

There are two types of electronic fish finders: echo sounders and sonars. Echo sounders are used to find fish which swim close to the sea-bed. Sound waves are sent out from the boat and echo back when they hit a shoal of fish or the bottom of the sea. Sonars send out sound waves around the boat to find fish which swim close to the sea's surface.

When the sound waves are broken by a shoal of fish, this is seen by the fisherman on a paper graph or a television-type screen. He then knows exactly where and when to 'shoot' his net into the water.

Modern technology helps to locate fish.

An echo sounder will also give a fisherman a picture of the sea-bed and will tell him whether it is hard or soft. This is important as some fish only live on hard ground, while others like soft ground. If the picture shows hard ground, a fisherman also knows he risks damaging his net.

While a boat has its net out catching fish, it will make a signal to other boats to keep away, in case they get tangled-up in it. This signal is usually a basket put up on top of the mast.

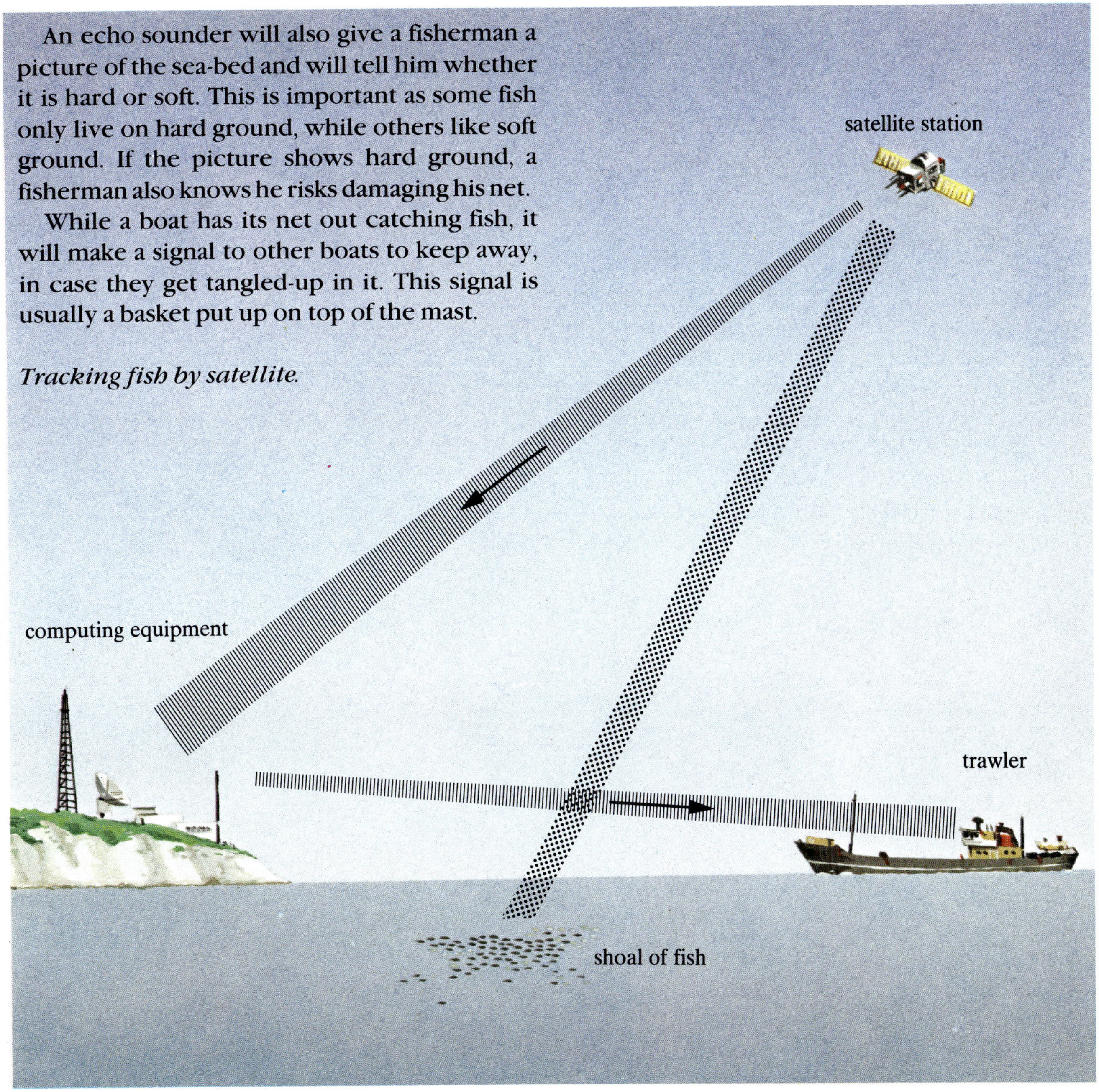

Tracking fish by satellite.

4. The main fishing methods

From the way they feed and swim, fish are divided into two main types: demersal and pelagic. Demersal fish, like cod, haddock, plaice and sole, swim deep down in the water, close to the sea-bed. Pelagic fish, like herring, mackerel, tuna and sardine, swim in the middle water, between the sea-bed and the surface.

The depth at which fish swim and feed is very important in the way they are caught.

Demersal fish are captured in trawls. These are nets dragged along the bottom of the sea by boats called trawlers. Trawl nets are funnel-shaped, with an entrance (mouth) into which the fish swim.

Big ball-shaped rollers, called bobbins, keep the bottom edge of the mouth on the sea-bed and help it move along. Across the top edge are large plastic floats which help the mouth to stay open.

To catch pelagic fish, nets called purse seines are used (see page 41). These are huge nets up to

Demersal fish are caught with trawl nets.

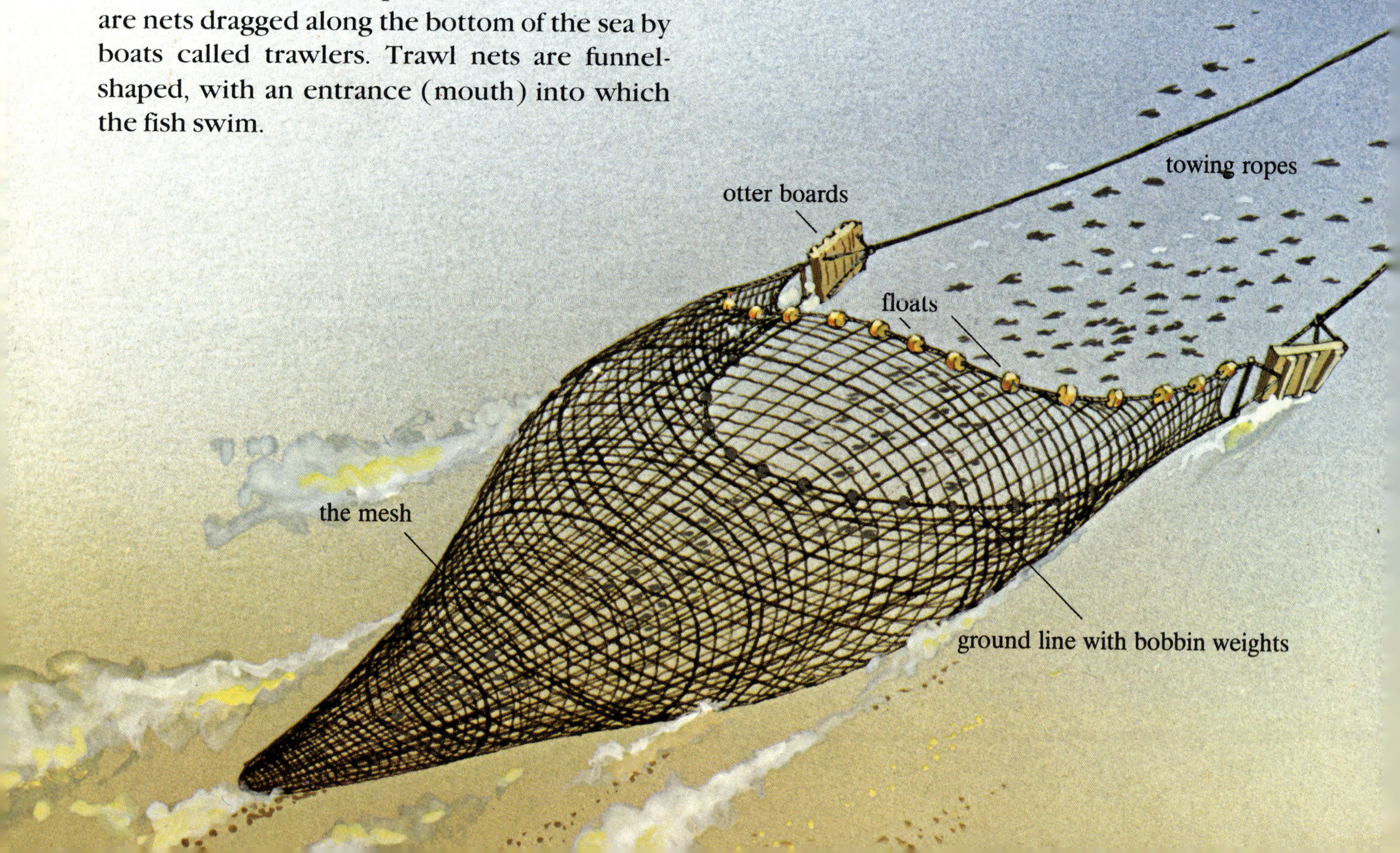

one and a half kilometres (one mile) around, which are used to encircle the fish like a lasso. When the fish are trapped, the net is closed, or 'pursed', and dragged towards the boat for unloading. Losing one of these nets can be very expensive for fishermen as they can cost up to £100,000 each.

Trawlers with special nets can be used to catch pelagic fish. But fish like mackerel and herring swim very fast, so such boats need powerful engines. To get the speed and a very wide spread of net, two boats are sometimes used to pull one net through the water.

Drawing in a fishing net in Germany.

5. Fishing boats of the world

From giant factory ships to dug-out canoes, fishing boats come in all shapes and sizes. They are built from wood, steel, plastic and sometimes even from cement.

Boats need to differ in size and shape to suit various local conditions and needs. In certain areas of India, Africa and South-East Asia the design of fishing methods and boats has evolved over thousands of years. Small, lightweight boats without engines are often most efficient in feeding villagers in hot countries where high protein food is difficult to obtain.

For the colder waters of the Atlantic and Arctic Oceans, where the sea can be very rough, much more sturdy ships are needed. Some of these use special equipment to break the ice.

In these waters it is the massive factory trawlers, from countries like the Soviet Union and

A Maltese fishing boat often has 'eyes'.

A Russian factory trawler and fish carriers.

The successful Kenyan fishing industry relies on boats of all sizes.

Poland, which are the giants of the ocean. These ships, up to 122 metres (400 feet) long, can gulp up hundreds of tonnes of fish.

There are even larger vessels called 'mother ships', which carry lots of small boats on board. These are lowered into the water, where they catch fish and supply the mother ship.

In the Pacific Ocean, fishing boats often carry helicopters on board, which fly ahead to spot the shoals of tuna fish.

Dinka tribesmen skilfully craft their boats from complete tree trunks.

6. Keeping fish fresh

The best time to eat a fish is as soon as it has come out of the sea. This is not often possible, because where we buy fish is often a very long way from where it was caught.

So how is it that we can eat fresh, tasty seafood, when the fish was caught many months before? This is because of immediate refrigeration, which is often done on the boat at sea, as soon as the fish is brought aboard.

Whole fish are packed into machines which freeze them into a solid block. Sometimes the fishermen remove the bones and cut off the heads of the fish first. This is called filleting. The fish is then stored in a special room which is kept very cold, so the fish does not thaw or melt

Fish on sale in Paris.

before it reaches port.

Once back on shore, the fish is put immediately into another cold store, where it is kept until the factory is ready to use it.

Even if fish is not frozen, fishermen have ways of keeping it fresh. They pack it in boxes and put flakes of ice all around it. This helps them get a better price at the market.

Sometimes fish are stored at sea in tanks filled with seawater kept at a very low temperature. The fish is not frozen solid, so this method is called 'chilling'.

Slabs of ice keep fish fresh at Billingsgate market in London.

7. Buying and selling seafood

Seafood is bought and sold many times during its journey from the sea to our tables. When a fisherman comes home to his port, he never knows how much money he will get. If there is a lot of fish to be sold, he will not do very well. If bad weather has stopped a lot of boats going out to fish, then he will get a good price.

Selling fish in a port starts very early in the morning. The boxes of fish from all the boats are displayed together around the market and auctioned. All the buyers gather round and shout out a price. The one who calls out the highest price gets the fish.

Weighing squid at a fish stall in China.

Above *A floating fish market in Istanbul.*

Above *Billingsgate is London's largest fish market.*

Some fish will be taken away to factories, where it is filleted and packed ready for the shops. Remaining fish will then start another journey to be sold at what are called inland markets. These are markets which are often in big cities, a long way from the sea. Again early in the morning, shopkeepers, fishmongers and restaurant owners come to the inland market to buy their fish.

Two of the most famous inland markets are Billingsgate in London and Rungis in Paris. These markets are also very popular with people from foreign countries who have come to live in these cities. They can buy all sorts of unusual fish from their homelands, which are specially brought in.

A fish auction in Yorkshire, England.

8. Dividing up the sea

For thousands of years the sea was a huge hunting ground where anyone could fish. But this changed in the 1970s. Now, each country with a coastline owns all the fish as far as 322 kilometres (200 miles) from its shores.

This happened because too much fish was being taken out of the sea. Some countries with only small fishing fleets found all their fish being taken by big ships from other countries. Sometimes this caused battles to take place over fish, like the 'cod wars' between Iceland and Britain (in 1958, 1972 and 1975), in which fishermen had to be protected by their navies.

To stop this happening, most of the fishing countries at the United Nations Law of the Sea Conference, in 1977, decided that each country

The world's major fishing areas.

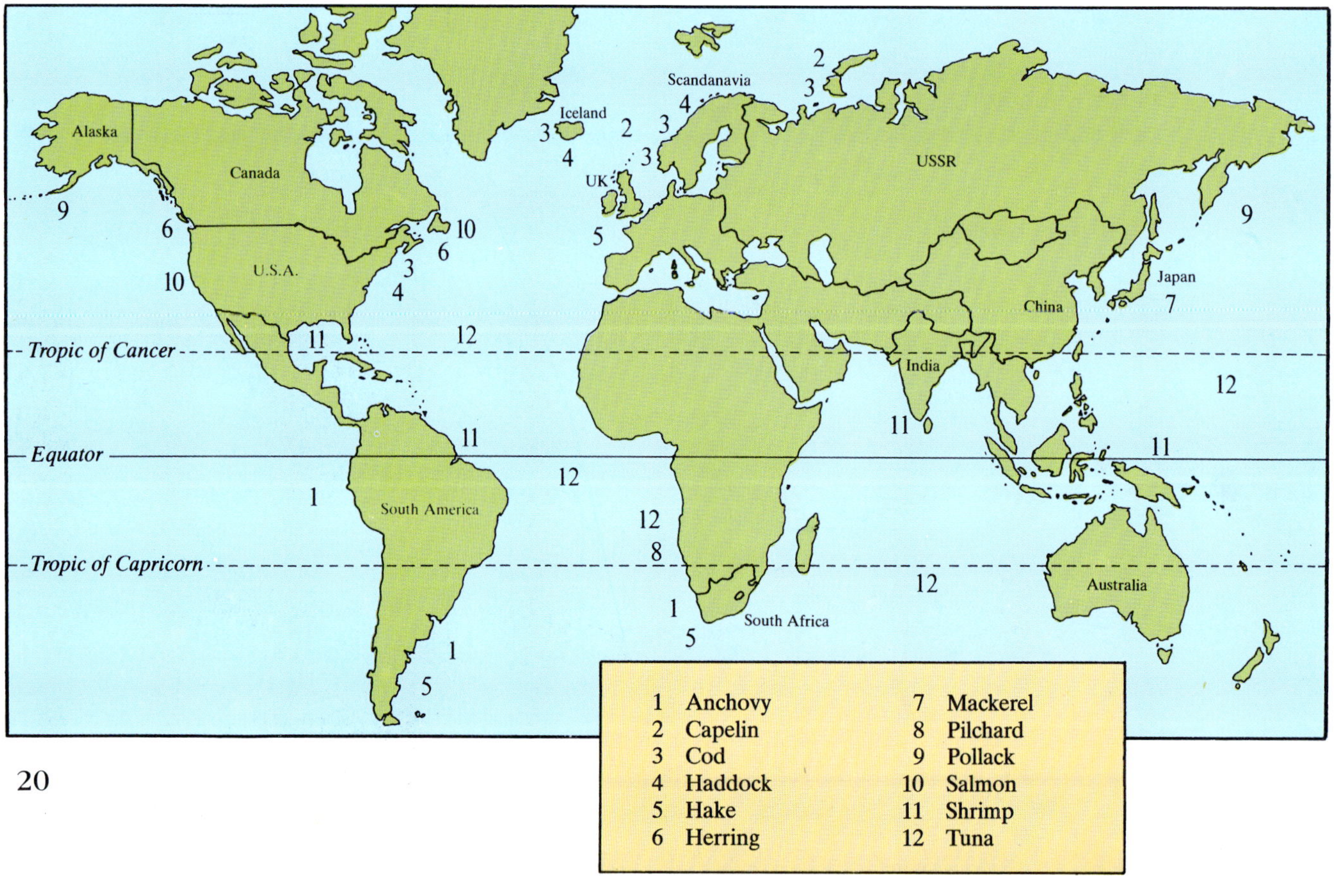

should have what is called a fishing limit. Where there is less than 322 kilometres (200 miles) of water separating countries, an imaginary line is drawn half way between them, which is called a median line.

Not all countries have enough boats or skill to catch all the fish in their limits. When this happens, they allow other countries to fish in their waters by selling them a licence.

Some of the less-developed fishing countries allow foreign boats into their waters, in return for letting their native fishermen work on them. This is one way new methods of fishing are learned and exchanged.

Right *In Brazil much fishing takes place along the Golden Coast.*

Below *A cod trawler unloading.*

9. Policing the sea

Just as on the land, there are policemen at sea, to keep law and order. Since the introduction of 322-kilometre (200-mile) fishing limits, almost every fishing country has special fleets of boats patrolling their waters to make sure that no intruders get in.

The British Royal Navy's Fishery Protection Squadron at work.

These police forces of the sea are known as protection fleets and are usually manned by people from the navy or coastguard. To patrol such a large area of sea is a difficult job and sometimes spotter planes are used. These fly over the sea and spot boats which may be illegally fishing. Their positions are then radioed to the patrol craft, which intercepts the boats. The captains of these patrol craft have the power to

arrest any boat and escort it to a port, where a judge can impose a fine for fishing illegally.

Watching over fishing limits is only part of the job of people in the protection fleet. Having boarded a boat, they have to check that the mesh in the nets is the correct size with a special gauge. They must also ensure that the boat does not have more than the allowed amount of fish on board.

The mesh in a fisherman's net must be large enough for young fish to escape.

The ways a fisherman can be punished for breaking the law at sea vary from country to country. Apart from paying a fine, he can have his catch taken away or be banned from fishing for life. In some cases, fishermen have even been put to death!

10. Sharing out the fish

Fishing limits are not enough to protect fish. Other ways have to be found so that there is enough for every country, without damaging the stocks of fish.

Every year scientists decide how much of each fish stock should be caught. This is called a Total Allowable Catch (TAC for short). This is then divided into a share for each country, which is known as a quota. Often there are arguments over sharing out the quotas, especially among EEC countries, many of whom use the North Sea as a hunting ground.

The system of quotas is very important because it is a way of making sure that there will be enough fish in the future. Fish have special areas in the sea where they breed, then when they are older they disperse around the oceans of the world. As they do not respect fishing limits, fish in these areas, or spawning grounds, have to be protected, so that they can grow and be caught later on.

While quotas can help the stocks to grow, there are also other regulations which fishermen must obey. The net carried on a boat must have holes in it big enough for baby fish to escape. These holes are known as the mesh.

Protecting fish, or conservation, as it is known, has become very important in recent years. In the past many fish stocks almost completely disappeared so fishing them had to be banned to give them time to increase again.

Norway is one of several countries that fish in the North Sea.

Young fish may be reared in a hatchery for protection.

11. Top fishing nations

Japan is the most powerful fishing nation in the world. Not only does it catch more fish than any other country, its people eat more fish than anyone else in the world. The Japanese fishing fleet now catches over 11 million tonnes of fish each year. The other two most important fishing countries are the Soviet Union, which catches over 9 million tonnes, and China with 5 million tonnes.

Both Japan and the Soviet Union catch almost every kind of fish and nowhere is too far for them to go. Both these countries have huge ships which can stay at sea for many months. These are really floating factories, which can put fish straight into tins or freeze it into solid blocks immediately it comes out of the sea.

When every country obtained a 322-kilometre (200-mile) fishing limit, many giant ships were stopped from fishing in their usual places. However, because they still need fish, these ships anchor out at sea and local boats transfer fish to them. This is called 'klondyking'.

Off the British coast, mackerel and herring are klondyked to factory ships from the Soviet Union and other Communist countries. Off the coasts of the USA and Canada, cod, hake and

A ship from Japan's large fishing fleet.

herring are transferred to foreign factory ships.

Since the fishing limits came into force, the USA has also become a very important fishing country, and is now the fourth largest in the world with a catch of over 4 million tonnes.

Above *Many Japanese recipes use fish.*

Below *The latest tuna fishing boats in the USA carry helicopters to fly ahead and spot fish.*

12. Seafood and health

The Dutch enjoy eating fish raw.

'We are what we eat' is an old saying. But it is one which has a lot of truth in it, certainly as far as the health of our bodies is concerned.

More and more people are eating fish and other foodstuffs from the sea. Over the past ten years, world sales of seafood have doubled, and are now worth over sixty million US dollars a year. As there are over 30,000 different types of fish, we need never get bored with it.

Apart from being tasty food to eat, seafood is good for us and helps our bodies to grow and be strong. Seafood contains important proteins which our bodies must have to produce energy and warmth. Fats, which the body also needs, come from the oil in seafood. Vitamins are another important benefit from seafood, especially vitamin A, which protects us against disease, and vitamin D which keeps bones and teeth strong.

As more people have become concerned with keeping healthy, so the demand for seafood has grown. Many doctors recommend seafood as an important part of our diet because it is low in animal fats, which often lead to heart disease. Studies have shown that people like the Inuit, whose main diet consists of seafood, very rarely suffer from heart disease.

Seafood is the main diet of the Inuit.

Seafood can also be important in controlling our weight, because compared with many other foods it is low in calories. Medical research into the foods we eat is really only just beginning, but already people are eating more seafood and less red meat.

Above *Seaweed is another nutritional food from the sea.*

Below *These women are demonstrating new ways to prepare fish.*

13. Farming fish

If we are to have enough fish in the future, we have to be sensible about how much we catch now. But there are ways of getting fish without taking them out of the sea: we can grow them!

Growing fish is called fish farming or aquaculture. This can be done in ponds or lakes and in cages in the sea. We have learned so much about this that 10 million tonnes of farmed fish are now being produced each year.

Fish farming starts with fish eggs. These are put into tanks of warm water until they hatch and become what is known as 'fry'. When the fry is strong enough, it is put into cages in the sea, where it is fed with small pellets until it is large enough for us to eat. On modern fish farms a computer is used to feed the fish at a special time each day.

Farmed fish grow much more quickly than wild fish in the sea. This is because they do not use much energy while swimming about in a small cage.

Salmon and trout are the most important types of fish for fish farming because they fetch a high price. However, many others, including sole, turbot and plaice, are also grown. Some shellfish grow very fast in warm climates, especially shrimp and prawns. Countries like Ecuador, in South America, and India are very successful at growing shellfish.

Although we still have a lot to learn about farming fish, it has already become a very important way to produce fish.

The cultivation of oysters in Brazil.

Feeding time at a fish farm in Kent, England.

14. Fisheries and research

Scientists are vital to the fishing industry. They can tell fishermen how much fish they can catch and where they can catch it. Scientists need laboratories to carry out their work and they take these to sea, in what are called research ships.

Fisheries research ships are floating laboratories which can also catch fish. Using all their equipment, scientists can get samples of young fish and estimate how long they will take to grow. This allows fishermen to plan ahead how much they will be able to catch in the future.

Scientists also find new stocks of fish for fishermen. They can work out whether there are enough to catch by following the fish to see the places where they live.

Fishermen and scientists often work together, in trying to find out where fish go. These are called 'tagging' experiments. This means that scientists catch fish, clip a small disc on them, and put them back in the sea while they are still alive. When fishermen catch these

A scientist engaged in fisheries research.

By tagging salmon, scientists can monitor their movements.

fish later on – sometimes thousands of kilometres away – they give the tags back to the scientist who can then tell how far the fish have travelled.

Fishermen do not always have the time to test new nets and new ways to catch fish. The scientist does a lot of this work for them.

Scientists who work in laboratories ashore spend part of their time finding new ways to prepare fish so that it is safe and good to eat.

15. Changing one fish into another

Although the search is always going on to find more fish, there are millions of tonnes caught which are not used. This is because the fish are not nice to look at, have a taste people do not like, or are difficult for machines in fish factories to handle.

This unwanted fish often ends up being ground down into fish meal. This is a powder which is used to fertilize the earth or to feed animals and poultry.

Because it is full of protein, new ways have to be found to interest people in unwanted fish. Already this is happening with a fish called Alaskan Pollack. Over 5 million tonnes of this soft white fish (the world's biggest catch) is taken out of the sea each year, but it used to be hard to sell. Now many people all over the world are eating it, but they do not know it!

This is because the Japanese invented a way of making it taste and look like shellfish. They gave it a soft pink colour, added chemicals to make it taste like crab and other shellfish, then squeezed it out through machines into all sorts of interesting shapes.

You will now see this fish in shops and supermarkets with names like 'Crab Sticks', 'Ocean Sticks', 'Ocean Bites' and 'King Crab Flakes'. These 'shellfish' dishes are especially popular in Britain and the USA.

Crab sticks are made from a plentiful white fish – the Alaskan Pollack.

Changing one fish into another is called 'Engineered Seafood' or 'Substitute Fish Products' and many people believe that we will be able to do this with all sorts of fish and food.

Waste fish on its way to be made into animal foodstuffs.

16. Different tastes

Many people grow up liking the fish they ate as children. Usually, these came from the waters around their country. Because fish can now be transported quickly around the world by land, sea and air, we are able to taste fish from many countries. But while people are now eating many different kinds of fish, most countries still have their own favourite seafood taste.

In the Western world, mainly the USA and Britain, frozen fish is very popular, especially fish fingers. These are made from white fish, mainly cod, cut into finger shapes and covered with crispy breadcrumbs. In many parts of the world, they are known as fish sticks.

Above *Fresh fish being cooked and sold in Instanbul harbour.*

Below *Preparing rollmop herrings.*

In Japan, people are used to eating raw fish. *Sashimi*, which is raw tuna, is very popular. The Japanese also eat *kamaboko* (fish sausages) and fish balls made from minced fish.

Raw fish is also popular in the Scandinavian countries, where it is marinated. This means that it is preserved in salt or vinegar and even

On this factory production line cod is being made into fish fingers.

sometimes wine and beer. If you have eaten rollmop herrings you will have tasted marinated fish. The hot Latin American countries take advantage of their climate to preserve fish. They eat *bacalao*, which is cod preserved in salt and dried in the sun.

The real luxury fish dish, which is eaten in all countries, is caviar, known as the 'millionaire's food'. It is made with the eggs taken from a fish called the sturgeon.

17. The wonderful world of shellfish

Some of the tastiest and most unusual fish come from the shellfish family. These creatures lead strange lives; some bury themselves in the mud, while others cling to rocks and some even change sex.

The shellfish family is divided into three main types: crustaceans, molluscs and cephalopods. Prawns, crabs and lobsters are crustaceans. Mussels, oysters and clams are molluscs, and octopus and squid are cephalopods.

Shellfish are caught in a lot of different ways: in trawls and traps with special bait inside and even sucked up out of the sea with special dredges.

The name 'shellfish' is used because all these creatures have a very hard shell-like skin or live inside shells for protection.

Paella is a popular dish made with shellfish and rice.

Above *Shellfish usually fetch a good price.*

The shellfish that changes sex is the prawn, which lives in the cold waters of the North Atlantic. After a year of life as a male, the prawn changes into a female and is able to carry eggs and have babies for the rest of its life.

These prawns also mate in a strange way. The female loses her protective shell and gives out a smell which attracts the male. When they have mated, the male stays with the female to guard her, until her shell grows again.

Fishermen like catching shellfish because they usually fetch a good price.

Above *The shrimp is a tasty shellfish.*

Below *Crabs catch and eat smaller fish.*

18. Sharing the sea

The sea is a wild place, but we are learning to tame it and get more and more of the things we need out of it. This means that fishermen have had to learn to share the sea with men who are taking oil and gas from under the sea-bed.

To get oil and gas out of the sea we have to build rigs. These are like mini-cities on stilts, where the oil men live and work. For fishermen these huge rigs mean that large parts of the sea can no longer be fished.

Because the sea is a difficult place to work in, oil equipment is often lost and fishermen catch their nets on it. Sometimes fishermen can claim money from the oil companies if they damage their nets or boats.

Fishermen are also trying to persuade the oil companies to bury all the pipes that carry oil under the sea-bed, so that when the oil runs out, the sea-bed will be clear again.

An oil rig must withstand rough seas.

The sea-bed also plays a part in letting us talk to people in other countries. Many telephone cables are carried across the bottom of the sea. Boats have to be careful to avoid these, when they are fishing, because they are very expensive to repair.

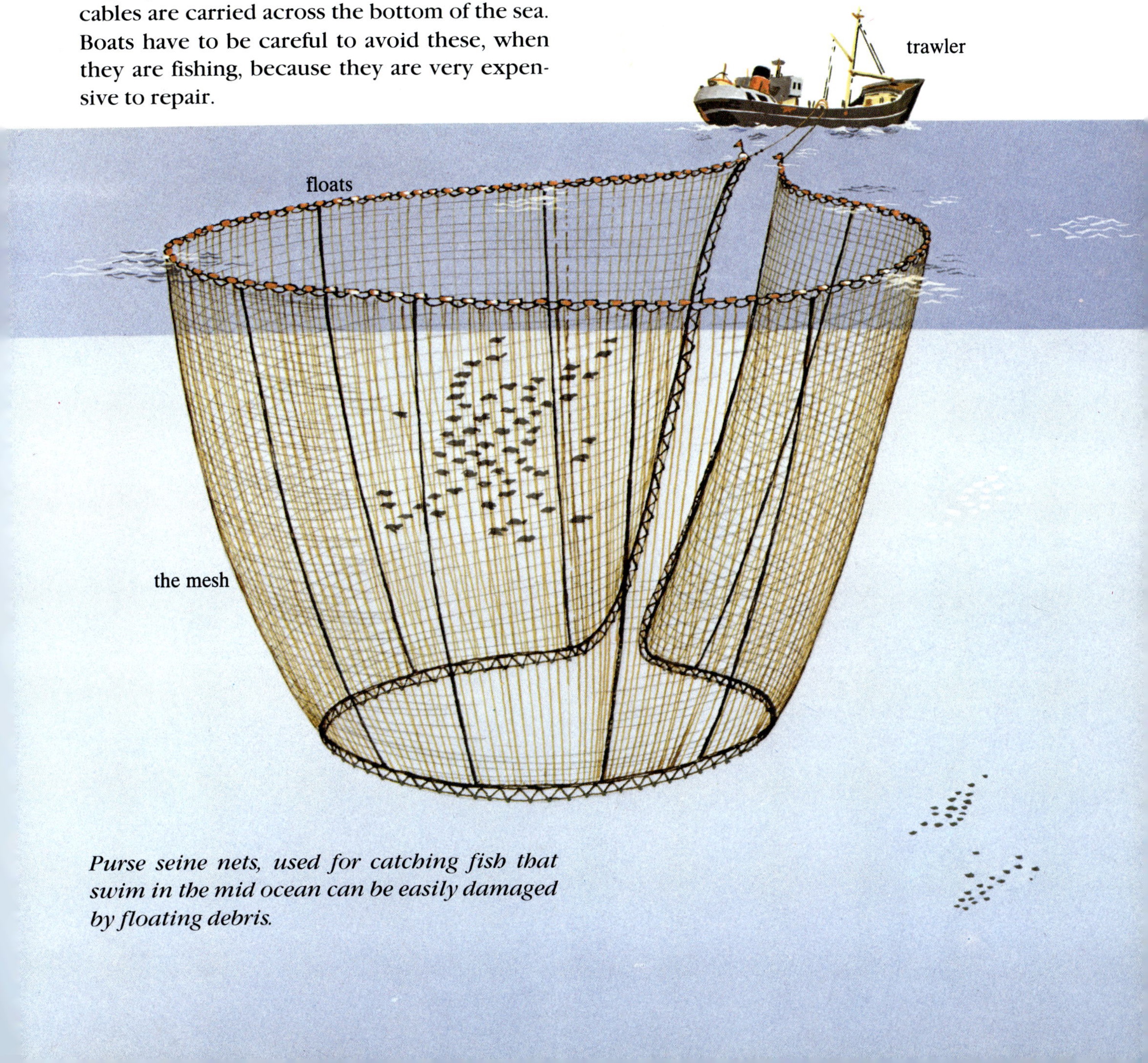

Purse seine nets, used for catching fish that swim in the mid ocean can be easily damaged by floating debris.

19. Keeping the sea clean

The sea is getting dirtier. This is because we are using it as a dustbin in which to put all our waste. Dumping things we do not want in the sea is known as pollution. This is a great danger to all the creatures that live in it and eat food from it.

Millions of fish die each year because things like nuclear waste, chemicals and sewage are being put into the sea. Carrying oil across the sea in huge tankers has killed a lot of life in the sea. Oil sometimes spills out for hundreds of kilometres when these ships have an accident. This kills not only fish and birds but also destroys plankton, which is the food fish eat.

Big patches of oil spilled into the sea are known as 'slicks'. These have to be dispersed as quickly as possible. One way to get rid of these slicks is to spray them with foam containing detergents. Another way is to put a floating wall around the slick to stop it spreading. This is often done to protect our beaches, along which many sea creatures live.

Even from the land we can pollute the sea. Spraying crops with chemicals to stop them becoming diseased means that many of these chemicals end up in rivers, which run out into the sea.

Pollution has become such a big problem that many countries now have laws to stop waste being put into the sea. People who are caught doing this have to pay big fines.

Pollution of the sea also affects life on land.

The army dispersing oil spilled on the seashore in France.

Facts and figures

Main Species of Fish Caught

Species	Catch in tonnes		
	1983	1982	1981
Alaska pollack	5,047,324	4,478,217	4,176,828
Japanese pilchard	4,219,677	3,966,090	3,613,379
Chilean pilchard	3,888,694	3,271,713	2,804,242
Capelin	2,554,162	1,844,639	2,805,095
Atlantic cod	2,070,366	2,225,791	2,345,845
Chilean jack mackerel	1,668,260	2,199,641	1,740,315
Chub mackerel	1,621,583	1,848,534	2,439,605
Atlantic herring	1,141,736	983,409	961,626
European pilchard	930,310	882,896	991,755
Gulf menhaden	923,585	854,336	552,587
Skipjack tuna	773,719	753,928	733,271
Largehead hairtail	766,670	796,260	733,271
European anchovy	735,255	703,969	701,336
Atlantic mackerel	611,585	624,633	635,798
Cape horse mackerel	571,911	666,068	623,713
Norway pout	548,013	532,526	346,004
Blue whiting	543,359	547,299	906,707
Yellowfin tuna	533,629	524,839	571,844
Pacific cupped oyster	525,148	488,454	487,726
Saithe (pollack)	491,242	511,049	478,773

World Fish Catch in 1983

Country	Tonnes	Country	Tonnes
Japan	11,250,000	Brazil	844,500
USSR	9,756,797	Iceland	839,244
China	5,213,261	France	784,004
USA	4,142,546	Malaysia	741,089
Chile	3,978,078	Poland	735,089
Norway	2,822,312	Bangladesh	728,500
India	2,520,000	Vietnam	710,000
South Korea	2,400,387	Burma	585,800
Thailand	2,250,000	Turkey	567,304
Indonesia	2,112,230	Nigeria	515,249
Denmark	1,862,130	Netherlands	503,275
Philippines	1,836,877	Morocco	439,895
Peru	1,486,815	Argentina	416,339
Canada	1,337,296	Pakistan	343,402
Spain	1,250,000	Faroe Islands	329,879
Mexico	1,070,045	Ecuador	307,288
S. Africa & Namibia	1,050,981	West Germany	305,620
Taiwan	985,000	Tanzania	272,498
United Kingdom	846,535	Sweden	265,586
WORLD TOTAL		**76,470,600 tonnes**	

Glossary

Aquaculture Growing fish in captivity.
Auction A place where fish is sold.
Bobbins The heavy ball-shaped rollers which help a trawl net travel over the sea-bed.
Caviar The eggs from a fish called the sturgeon.
Demersal The name for fish which live on the bottom of the sea.
Echo sounder An electronic device for finding fish near the sea-bed.
Factory ship A trawler which processes its catch at sea. The fish it catches are sorted into sizes, washed, gutted, filleted and deep-frozen.
Filleting Taking the bones out of fish.
Fishing limit An area of sea around the coast which belongs to a country. Boats from other countries are not allowed to fish within these limits unless they have permission.
Fishmeal Ground and dried fish in powder or pellet form. It is rich in protein and is used to feed animals and to fertilize crops.
Floats Air-filled balls which keep the trawl net open.
Fry Baby fish.
Harpoon A spear used to catch whales.
Klondyking Selling fish at sea.
Marinated Fish preserved in vinegar or salt.
Mother ship A giant ship which carries small fishing boats on its deck.
Pelagic The name for fish which swim near the surface.
Purse seining Encircling a shoal of fish with a net which can be closed like a purse, using a rope 'fastener', to trap the fish.
Shooting Casting the net into the sea.
Slick A patch of oil on the sea.
Sonar An electronic device for finding fish swimming near the surface.
Rig A platform used to take oil out of the sea.

Sources of further information

More information on the fishing industry can be obtained from:

Sea Fish Industry Authority
10 Young Street
Edinburgh EH2 4JQ
Scotland

Seafish Information Service
144 Cromwell Road
London SW7 4EF

Irish Sea Fisheries Board
Crofton Road
Dun Laoghaire
Dublin
Eire

EEC Fisheries Commission
200 rue de la Loi
1049 Brussels
Belgium

National Marine Fisheries Service
US Department of Commerce
National Oceanic and Atmospheric Administration
Washington DC 20235
USA

Books to read

Encyclopedia of Fish (Octopus Books)
FAIRCLOUGH, C. *A Day with a Fisherman* (Wayland)
HANSON, D. F. *Fishing Boats and Fisher Folk* (Dent)
MILTON, B. *Fishing Boat* (Black)
SWAYNE, R. & SAVAGE, P. *I am a Fisherman* (Dent)

Nearly one hundred technical books on fishing are published by Fishing News Books Ltd., 1 Long Garden Walk, Farnham, Surrey.

Picture acknowledgements

The author and publishers would like to thank the following for allowing illustrations to be reproduced in this book: Anthony Blake Photo Library 17, 19 (left); 'BARNABY'S PICTURE LIBRARY' *cover*, 32; Bord Iascaigh Mhara (Irish Sea Fisheries Board) 29 (bottom), 36 (left); *frontispiece*, 36 (right), T.E. Clark 30, John Egan 18 (right), Julian Hall 6, all from Camerapix Hutchison Library; Esso 40; Fishing News International 10, 14 (right), 27 (bottom), 19 (right), 24, 25, 34, 37; Richard Kemp 15 (bottom), Nellaine Price 39 (bottom right), Jeff Simon 9 (top left), Colin Wilson 7 (left), all from Survival Anglia; TOPHAM 7 (right), 9 (top right), 14 (left), 16, 22, 26, 28 (both), 29 (top), 31, 33, 39 (top left and top right), 42, 43; Royal Navy Fishery Protection Squadron 23; Wayland Picture Library 13 (bottom), 15 (top), 18 (left), 21 (both), 27 (top), 35, 38. The illustrations on pages 8, 9, 11, 12, 13, 20 and 41 are by Malcolm S. Walker.

Index

Alaskan Pollack 34
Aquaculture 30, 46
Arctic Ocean 14
Atlantic Ocean 14, 39

Bacalao 37
Billingsgate 19
Bobbins 12, 46
Britain 20, 26, 34
Buying fish 18

Caviar 37, 46
'Chilling' fish 17
'Cod wars', The 20–21
Conservation 7, 24

Demersal fish 12, 46

Echo sounders 10–11, 46
EEC 24
'Engineered Seafood' 34

Factory ships 26–7, 46
Facts and figures 44–5
Farming fish 30
Filleting 16, 46
Fishing boats 14–15
Fishing limit 21–24, 26–27, 46
Fish markets 19
Fishmeal 34, 46
Fishing methods 12–13

Gas 40

Harpoon 8, 46
Hunting fish 7–11

Iceland 20

Japan 26, 34, 36

Kamaboko 36
'Klondyking' 26, 46

Median line 21
Mesh 24
'Mother ships' 15, 46

North Atlantic prawn 39
North Sea 24

Oil 9, 40–42

Pacific Ocean 15
Pelagic fish 11–13, 46
Pollution 42
Protection fleets 22–3
Purse seines 12, 46

Research ships 32
Rungis 19

Sashimi 36
Seafood 28–9
Selling fish 19
Shellfish 38–9
Slicks 42, 46
Sonars 10, 46
Soviet Union 15, 26
Storing fish 16–17
'Substitute Fish Products' 34

TAC 24
'Tagging' experiments 32–3
Tankers 42
Trawlers 12–15
Trawl nets 12

United Nations Law of the Sea Conference 20–21
USA 26–7, 34, 36